A Young Citizen's Guide To:

Voluntary Groups

Patricia Levy

HODDER
Wayland
An imprint of Hodder Children's Books

A Young Citizen's Guide series

Parliament
Local Government
The Electoral System
Central Government
The Criminal Justice System
Voluntary Groups
The Media in Politics
The European Union
Political Parties
Money

Published in Great Britain in 2002 by Hodder Wayland,
an imprint of Hodder Children's Books

Editor: Patience Coster
Series editor: Alex Woolf
Series design: Simon Borrough
Picture research: Glass Onion Pictures
Consultant: Dr Stephen Coleman

British Library Cataloguing in Publication Data
    Levy, Patricia, 1951-
    A young citizen's guide to voluntary groups
    1. Associations, institutions, etc. - Great Britain -
    Juvenile literature
    I. Title II. Voluntary Groups
    361.7'63'0941

ISBN 0 7502 3779 1

Printed and bound in Hong Kong
by C&C

Hodder Children's Books,
a division of Hodder Headline
Limited, 338 Euston Road,
London NW1 3BH

Picture acknowledgements:
the publisher would like to
thank the following for
permission to use their
pictures: James Davis Travel
Photography 6; Eye
Ubiquitous 29 (Paul Seheult);
Impact 10 (Alex
MacNaughton), 22 (Anne-
Marie Purkiss); PA Photos 27
(Shaun Flannery); Popperfoto
20 (Andy Clark);
Popperfoto/Reuters 18 (top,
Ian Hodgson), 19, 25
(Jonathan Evans); Press
Association/Topham
contents page (Chris Bacon);
28 (Tim Ockenden);
Topham/ImageWorks 16;
Topham Picturepoint 4, 5, 11,
12-13, 15, 26; Topham/Press
Association 7 (Michael
Stephens), 8-9 (Neil Munns),
14 (Fiona Hanson), 18
(bottom, Chris Bacon), 21
(Tony Harris), 23 (William
Conran), 24 and *title page*
(Neil Munns); Wayland Picture
Library 17.

Cover: Crisis boy with food
(Topham); hearing dog for the
deaf (RSPCA, AHAM); villagers
and Greenpeace (Popperfoto).

Contents

Pamela Ross holds her daughter, Alison, at the launch of the Dunblane Ribbon, a voluntary group dedicated to helping children caught up in conflict and violence around the world.

What are Voluntary Groups? ☒

Voluntary groups are active in all aspects of the UK's social and economic life. There are about 300,000 in the UK, ranging from neighbourhood chess clubs to influential, international organizations such as Oxfam. In between are thousands of voluntary groups with vastly different structures, aims, memberships and incomes. What links them all is that they operate independently of the government or the businesses that might donate money to them. The voluntary sector of society is often called the third sector; the other two are government and business.

Registered charities

Unlike private companies, voluntary groups do not exist to make a profit. Many voluntary groups (though not all) are registered charities, this means that they are registered with the Charity Commission (England and Wales - see page 6) or with the Inland Revenue or DHSS (Scotland and Northern Ireland). A charity is an organization set up to help those in need. Any voluntary group with an income of more than £1,000 a year should register as a charity, although there is no penalty for not registering. There are some advantages to registering as a charity. They are:

- the gaining of charitable status, which means that a voluntary group pays less tax on its income than a private company;
- credibility – registered charities are seen by the public as well-organized, legally trustworthy and worth donating money to;
- legal protection – should the group go into debt or be sued, it is protected by the laws governing charitable bodies.

An Amnesty International protestor. Amnesty campaigns on behalf of people's human rights in countries in which these rights are ignored. As a voluntary group, it does not receive financial support from the government.

However, there are some disadvantages to having charitable status, as follows:

- the voluntary group is not allowed to campaign in favour of one political party or another;
- it is subject to trading restrictions (in other words, it is only allowed to devote a small amount of its time and resources to trading);
- its activities are monitored by the Charity Commission.

Under these circumstances, unusual situations may arise. For example, a private, fee-paying school like Eton is a registered charity while Amnesty International, a public group open to everyone, is not. This is because Amnesty campaigns about issues concerning attacks on basic human rights, for example, the death penalty. Amnesty's role means that it often has to criticize governments. It cannot therefore be restricted by Charity Commission rules that say it should not make political statements.

Voluntary groups – facts and figures, May 2001

- **80 per cent of UK voluntary groups have no paid staff, but are run by volunteers.**
- **188,000 of the UK's voluntary groups are registered charities.**
- **30,000 registered charities pay wages to their administration staff.**
- **2,300 recreation grounds, 2,400 parent teacher associations and 5,300 village halls are registered charities.**
- **600 charities in the UK are dedicated to cancer relief.**
- **200 charities in London are dedicated to helping the homeless.**

Eton school is not a voluntary group. However, it benefits from being a registered charity.

5

If a voluntary group wishes to be accepted as a charity, it must fulfil one or more of a range of conditions. To be accepted as a charity, a voluntary group must help the poor, the handicapped or the aged, or it must further the advancement of religion or education, or it must serve other purposes of benefit to the community. Most charities qualify under the last option.

The Charity Commission
The Charity Commission oversees charities and is concerned with their reform. It is funded by the government but is independent of it. Five commissioners and their teams of lawyers, accountants and experts in the field of voluntary work maintain the public register of charities (the list of voluntary groups that have registered with the Commission) and investigate misconduct, for example, the misuse of charity funds. The Charity Commission also advises charity trustees, the people who oversee the administration of individual charities, and investigates ways of making the administration of charities more efficient and less expensive.

The history of volunteering
The earliest official form of voluntary public service was probably provided by almshouses. These were buildings financed by public donation where the sick and needy could find food and shelter. The first almshouses were set up a thousand years ago by individuals, churches or by local villages and towns. However, during the sixteenth century, thousands of church communities were destroyed, along with their almshouses.

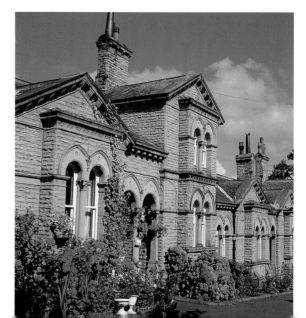

Many almshouses survive today, offering sheltered accommodation to older people.

In the nineteenth century, vast numbers of people flocked to the growing towns and cities in search of work. During this period of industrial revolution, there was a marked increase in poverty in towns and cities. Some wealthy industrialists used part of their fortunes for the public good. These 'philanthropists' established foundations and charities, many of which still survive today (see Chapter 2).

What do voluntary groups do?

Modern voluntary groups have three chief activities: campaigning, providing funds and providing services. Most of them perform all of these activities, while some are dedicated to just one or two. Greenpeace, for example, campaigns on behalf of the environment and raises funds in order to do so. It does not, however, provide a service for the environment beyond its campaigning activities. Other charities are geared more towards providing services, such as accommodation for the homeless, information for people with particular illnesses, or assistance to the disabled. They are funded by endowments (large sums of money donated by wealthy people) or local government grants rather than by public donations.

Greenpeace campaigners on the River Thames in London, bringing attention to the dangers of shipping plutonium.

How are Voluntary Groups Funded?

Voluntary groups find their money from a variety of sources. There are 2,500 grant-making trusts in the UK, giving grants of over £900 million a year to charities, for medical research, to students, to needy individuals and more. These trusts are themselves registered charities and most receive their income from an endowment. One such trust is the Boots Charitable Trust, which gives financial help to students and charities.

Local authorities give £600 million a year to locally based groups, such as community or sports centres. Government departments provide another £500 million to national groups, such as the AIDS charities. Various businesses, about 1,500 in all, donate £270 million in sponsorship, loans of equipment, and the free use of premises. Since it was set up in 1995, the National Lottery Charity Fund has donated £1.75 billion to 35,000 voluntary groups.

Some voluntary groups rely on public donations as a major source of income. During the last decade there has been an overall decline in the amount of money donated to charity by the public. (This may be because many people believe that their money is donated indirectly via the National Lottery.) As a charity grows in size, the cost of running the organization drains a greater proportion of its income. Big charities have on their staff well-paid professionals who run campaigns designed to increase public donations. One such large-scale campaign was a series of hard-hitting advertisements for Barnardo's in the national newspapers. (Barnardo's is a charity that works to prevent child abuse, among other things.)

Other smaller charities, for example, the charity Children in Distress, rarely run such campaigns and receive much of their income from collection boxes or from charity shops run by volunteer workers. These smaller charities have been the most disadvantaged by the overall decline in income from donations.

Red Nose Day

Since 1985, the voluntary group Comic Relief has generated £250 million for charity. On Red Nose Day, many celebrities give up a great deal of their time to urge people to donate money to charity. On BBC 1, television programmes are dedicated almost completely to fund-raising events. But some people have questioned whether society should encourage us to expect something in return for our charitable donations, whether it is an evening's television-watching or auctioned-off personal items from a celebrity. In particular, many people found it disturbing that British Telecom should have made a profit of £280,000 (excluding Value Added Tax) during the Celebrity Big Brother show that was shown as part of Red Nose Day on Channel 4 television. A government body, the Monopolies Commission, does not allow BT to show preference to any of its customers, so the telephone company had to charge Channel 4 the standard rate for the premium lines it set up for the voting.

The comedian Lenny Henry celebrates Red Nose Day with a group of children.

Funding and policy-making Voluntary
groups receive funds from members of the public,
businesses and local and national government. In
many cases they do this in exchange for performing
certain functions, such as running a sports centre
or village hall, providing care for the homeless (like
Shelter) or providing assistance for sufferers of
particular illnesses (like Lighthouse, which helps
AIDS sufferers).

However, carrying out these functions may cause
conflicts of interest. For example, members of the
public who donate to charities see them as
institutions independent of government, which fulfil
a certain role because it is their social and moral
responsibility, not because they are paid by
government to do so. But, increasingly, funds are
awarded as contracts in which the government lays
out certain conditions that the charity must fulfil in
order to receive funding. The charity or voluntary
group then becomes obliged to carry out those
exact conditions as its part of the arrangement.

When this occurs, the charity or voluntary group
cannot easily alter its goals or change policies, even
though the interests of those being helped might be
better served by doing so. For example, one of the
charities that helps the homeless could be
contracted to provide an individual with hostel
accommodation even though the person
concerned might benefit more from the
downpayment on a bedsit, or might simply be
unable to cope with the noise and fuss of a hostel.

A volunteer helps out in the
kitchen at a shelter for
homeless people.

The demands of business Frequently,
businesses that contribute to charities expect to
have one of their employees on the governing body
of the charity. Again, this may lead to conflicts of

interest. Businesses do not donate to charities solely out of kindness, but to attract good publicity. The employee of the donor business might feel obliged to influence the policy of the charity to the benefit of his or her company, rather than for the people the charity helps.

Charity law protects charities from the demands of their donors – in other words, they cannot do things their donors want them to do if these conflict with the interests of those being helped by the charity. Two charities, the Refugee Council and Shelter, are good examples of charities that have resisted the influence of their donors. Both have criticized government policy, despite the fact that they receive funding from government. They have been able to do this because of their secure reputation as caring and trustworthy organizations.

'Charities, in a sense, are the conscience of the nation and we must be allowed to follow our consciences. We should get funding on the basis of whether our projects make a difference. Money should not be contingent [dependent] on agreeing with government policies.'
Shaks Gosh, an executive of the charity Crisis, which provides emergency shelter for rough sleepers.

Children visit a display organized by the Refugee Council, a voluntary group dedicated to helping political refugees in the UK.

Grant-making trusts

A major source of funding for voluntary groups comes from grant-making trusts and foundations. These have a limited amount of cash to provide and only make donations in certain areas. (The Wellcome Trust, for example, makes grants only for medical research.) Most of them give one-off grants rather than annual ones, and for this reason few voluntary groups can survive on them.

Some of the grant-making trusts and foundations were set up in the nineteenth and twentieth centuries by wealthy philanthropists such as George Cadbury, who founded the Cadbury chocolate company. In 1894, Cadbury created and built a village near Birmingham for the employees of his chocolate factory. Called Bourneville, the 1,000-acre village with 3,500 dwellings had its own social security programme, pleasant houses and large gardens. Bourneville became part of the Cadbury Trust, set up in 1900 to provide healthy homes for a range of classes of people. The village still exists today.

Cadbury's brother, William, founded another charitable trust that makes donations to voluntary groups including churches, hospitals, medical research establishments, counselling services, educational institutions, museums and organizations working with offenders around Birmingham and abroad. Another nineteenth-century philanthropist, Jesse Boot, founded Nottingham University, created public parks, built almshouses for war veterans and set up the Boots

Following in the footsteps of the nineteenth-century philanthropists, multi-millionaire businessman Bill Gates visits a schools' project to which he has given financial support.

Charitable Trust which still makes grants to voluntary groups in the Nottingham area.

In modern times, the idea of philanthropy remains strong in the minds of the wealthy. Bill Gates, the founder of Microsoft, has set up a foundation that gives funds to a range of organizations (including voluntary ones) in education and medical research. A considerable amount of Gates' money has been granted to UK research institutions.

Mailshots
One way of finding long-term donors is by organizing mailshots – sending letters to people in their homes. In these letters the voluntary group explains its aims and asks for financial assistance. Mailshots are very expensive and use a lot of the money that people have donated. They also tend to be less effective each time they are used because potential donors become tired of the enormous amount of unsolicited mail they receive each day.

Campaigning is a major activity for many voluntary groups. They campaign in order to bring attention to their cause, to change public opinion and government policy and to attract donations and volunteers. Campaigns are usually aimed at large numbers of people. In cases where campaigning is aimed at a selected group, such as Members of Parliament, it is called lobbying. All sorts of groups, not just voluntary ones, are involved in lobbying.

In London, 1995, a protestor hands a leaflet to Shell Oil company chairman, John Jennings. The protest was against the oil company's policy in Nigeria at that time.

Voluntary groups campaign across the country using mass leafleting. (This is where leaflets are handed to people in the street, or included with the daily newspaper, or pushed through letterboxes by volunteers.) They also campaign using mailshots, newspaper advertisements, street collections, exhibitions in public places, petitions, and by setting up web sites and much more.

On a local level, groups campaign in a similar way but on a smaller scale. Perhaps they will use a float at a carnival, street petitions, street theatre, or stunts such as draping a banner in a prominent place. Sometimes they stage a demonstration when a public figure is with the press. An example of this is an incident that occurred during the 2001 general election campaign when a member of a voluntary group, seeking to draw attention to his cause, provoked the Deputy Prime Minister to violence.

The Ramblers Association

One voluntary group that successfully merges its local campaign groups with its national one is the Ramblers Association. This is essentially a social group arranging walks, slide shows and other activities for members with a common interest in walking and in local nature and history.

The Association's rare campaigns are aimed chiefly at keeping public footpaths accessible and preventing landowners from blocking rural walks. If a particular walk is obstructed deliberately, the local association takes up the cause by lobbying councillors, publicizing what has happened and maybe staging mass walks across the route. Since the Ramblers Association has the law on its side, these activities are often sufficient to have the footpath reopened. If local action fails, then the national organization steps in, taking the offending landowner to court and issuing press releases to make an issue of the case.

The Ramblers Association is a charitable organization with local groups throughout the UK. Its members enjoy the company of other walkers, have a healthy outdoor pastime and help to keep ancient footpaths open.

15

A son with his mother, an Alzheimer's sufferer. People with Alzheimer's disease lose many of their memories and find it difficult to look after themselves. The Alzheimer's Society helps families affected by the disease to cope with daily life.

Specific groups Some voluntary groups concentrate solely on their members' interests and find they are competing for the same, limited resources with other organizations. Housing associations, for example, compete against one another for funds, as do the charities concerned with homelessness in London. The Alzheimer's Society is an example of a voluntary group dedicated to the needs of a specific group, those people suffering from Alzheimer's disease and their family members who care for them at home. The Alzheimer's Society provides information, services and networking for carers, and funding for research into the disease. It also lobbies MPs and others on behalf of its members.

Rough sleepers

Charities competing for scarce resources include those that help people who sleep rough in towns and cities because they do not have their own homes. Each of these charities has a different approach to the problem, from supplying meals and beds to trying to find permanent accommodation and helping with the emotional and social problems of homeless individuals. Each form of assistance has its own administration costs. All these voluntary groups receive their funding from government sources and make very little from public donation. In 2000, the government mounted a campaign to encourage rough sleepers into permanent accommodation. At the same time, the government agency in charge of homelessness began its own campaign, advising people not to give money directly to homeless people but to donate it to one of the charities instead.

A voluntary group in Bristol has developed a different approach. The Aspire group is a non-profit-making organization, just like other charities, but it is financially independent of government funds or charitable donations. It employs homeless people in its business of catalogue sales. The business trains and gives full-time, well-paid work to people who can then find accommodation and hopefully, once settled, move on to other employment.

There are hundreds of charities dedicated to helping people such as this man, who have no permanent home and sleep rough in the streets. Many of these people have problems that go far beyond not having a home, and the charities try to deal with these as well as providing shelter.

Ethical campaigning Instead of seeking to assist a specific group of people, some voluntary organizations campaign in a more general way on moral or political grounds. Many people see campaigning as a good way of expressing their ethical and political concerns. Some find it more effective than relying on MPs and the parliamentary system. This kind of campaigning emerges in single-issue events such as the Countryside Coalition's campaigns in favour of blood sports, or the demonstrations by fuel protestors in autumn 2000 over the rising price of petrol. There are many examples of single-issue events, including protests over the poll tax and nuclear weapons during the 1980s and concerning the export of live animals for slaughter during the 1990s.

In autumn 2000, a series of protests against price of fuel led to blockades on UK motorwa and brought petrol stations to a close.

Amnesty International

One important campaigning voluntary group is Amnesty International. Amnesty is not a registered charity and seeks all its income from advertising campaigns and membership fees. When Amnesty plans a campaign to bring an issue before the public, it calls on all its members worldwide to do so.

ABACHA GOVERNMENT KILLS INNOCENT PEOPLE

In 1995, the Nigerian government sentenced nine environmental protestors to death. Amnesty urged its volunteers to try and stop the executions. It organized vigils (left) outside Nigerian embassies across the world. The campaign was unsuccessful, however, and the nine protestors were executed.

Amnesty members do not campaign against injustices in their own countries, only about issues in other countries. This is to avoid protestors becoming caught up in the injustices themselves, and to ensure that Amnesty's chief campaigners do not appear to be directly benefiting from its campaigns.

Diana, Princess of Wales, was a famous campaigner against landmines. She brought them to the attention of the world's media, and her death made many people feel that the landmine issue should be resolved in memory of her work.

Landmines
The issue of landmines has come to the world's attention through the activities of voluntary groups. During the 1990s, the demand to ban all manufacture of anti-personnel landmines grew until, in December 1997, an international treaty was introduced banning all anti-personnel landmines. The issue seemed to have been settled for everyone's good. However, when voluntary groups looked at the details of the treaty they found that it did not ban the use of anti-tank landmines, which continue to be manufactured. Many anti-tank landmines are more lethal to people than anti-personnel landmines.

Campaigning outside the law

Groups that campaign on moral issues are generally confined in their activities by the laws that govern them. Voluntary groups like charities are liable to prosecution if they support an action that results in public disorder or injury. They must also avoid presenting an exaggerated impression of the scale or nature of the problems they wish to highlight.

Some people feel so concerned about certain issues that they are prepared to break the law in order to attract publicity for their cause. Anti-capitalism demonstrations in Seattle, Gothenberg, Genoa and other cities are examples of this. Such protests, however, attract large numbers of peaceful protestors who seek to demonstrate their concern over what they see as the abuse of power by international private companies.

The scale of the protests appears to be having some effect, if only to ensure that some international businesses present themselves more carefully as organizations with a compassionate concern for the less fortunate. The scrutiny of protestors occasionally encourages organizations to

Anti-capitalism demonstrations have resulted in chaos in many cities around the world and in the deaths of two protestors. But they have also drawn attention to the exploitation of the developing world by huge, multinational companies.

Swords into Ploughshares

In 1996, a group consisting mainly of women from the anti-war group Swords into Ploughshares broke into a Royal Air Force military base and attacked a British Trident jet aeroplane, causing some damage. They did this because they felt they had no choice. The jet was about to be delivered to the Indonesian government, which was waging a war against a sector of its own people. Because their action was a campaigning gesture, the protestors willingly handed themselves over to the authorities. When they came to trial the jury acquitted them, accepting their defence that they caused the damage in order to prevent worse harm, a 'lawful excuse' under Common Law in Britain. The trial gained far more publicity than the attack on the aircraft and brought the British government under scrutiny for selling arms to a disreputable regime.

change their tactics. Oxfam and Christian Aid, two multimillion-pound charities, have recently chosen to withdraw their pension funds from tobacco and nuclear power companies and invest them in companies that are not criticized for the nature of the products they manufacture.

Voluntary groups such as Compassion in World Farming have brought attention to the export of live animals for slaughter in inhumane conditions.

Finding finance and bringing the needs of their beneficiaries to public attention are only two of the functions of voluntary groups. An increasing number of charities and non-profit-making organizations also provide services for their beneficiaries. Besides lobbying on behalf of its members, the Alzheimer's Society provides time for carers to take a rest from their demanding responsibility of looking after a family member on a full-time basis. Shelter provides practical assistance for the homeless, including temporary accommodation, blankets and food.

The Royal National Lifeboat Institution provides services to ships in distress in British waters. Its volunteer crews regularly risk their own lives in rescue missions.

A voluntary group whose chief function is the provision of services is the Royal National Lifeboat Institution (RNLI). Its funding and daily running are completely voluntary. As its income comes entirely

AIDS charities

Like homeless charities, there are a large number of AIDS charities operating in the UK. They compete for scarce government funding, and also have to contend with the public perception that less money is needed for AIDS because advances in medicine mean that the disease is under control. While the voluntary groups are receiving fewer donations, the number of HIV sufferers (HIV is the virus which causes AIDS) is increasing, even though deaths from AIDS are falling. The two largest AIDS charities, the Terence Higgins Trust and Lighthouse, have recently merged in an effort to reduce administration costs.

from public donations, it is not concerned with campaigning or lobbying or approaching businesses for funds. Unpaid staff and crew run the 223 lifeboat stations in the UK and Ireland, and there are 2,000 fundraising groups. A similar organization, the Guide Dogs for the Blind voluntary group, is funded by donations and its members are largely unpaid. Its service is to train and rear dogs for blind people and it achieves this with the help of volunteers at several training centres.

Complex administration For other

service providers, the structure of their organization and the issues involved are much more complex. The many homeless charities, for example, are largely concerned with providing a service, but their administration is complicated by the fact that there are a number of these groups and they rely heavily on government funding. Most of them have full-time, paid staff whose job it is to raise funds from the public or the government. Some of these groups receive funds in the form of government contracts, so they must negotiate exactly what services they are to provide. Campaigning on behalf of the homeless in the face of changing government policies is also a large part of their role.

Celebrities, such as Sarah Cawood and Gail Porter (pictured above) help to bring attention to charities such as the Terence Higgins Trust and their work in the voluntary sector.

Working in the Voluntary Sector

Of the thousands of people working in the voluntary sector, many of them are not volunteers at all but fully-paid career professionals with administrative, campaigning and personnel skills who choose to be employed by voluntary groups. Sometimes people work as volunteers in the voluntary sector because it is a good career move. Businesses tend to see volunteers as people who possess good time-management and other skills: they are able to do their job and volunteer their time; they possess extensive experience beyond their regular employment; and they are team-spirited people and good leaders.

Many volunteers also get a deep sense of giving something to the community and making a difference. Others find their way into voluntary work because they believe it is the best way to demonstrate their concern for particular issues in which they feel politicians are not interested. There is evidence to suggest that people who participate in voluntary work are happier and more trusting than people who do not.

This man is making a sponsored boat journey up the River Thames on behalf of the Cystic Fibrosis Trust.

Trustees Many people volunteer to act as the trustees of a charity. This means that they take part in the business administration, produce a report each year, perhaps act as treasurer and generally plan ahead and oversee how the charity is run. Because of the charity laws, this is a challenging job, as trustees may be held personally liable if the charity goes bankrupt or fails to meet its debts. Trustees can, however, insure themselves against such actions and many people who become trustees find voluntary work very rewarding.

Celebrities In a market where too many charities are competing for scarce donations, charities often find that the support of a famous person gives them an advantage over other voluntary groups. They approach popular television personalities who may have been personally affected by the issues that the charity represents – for example, a celebrity who may have had a mother with breast cancer, or a child with a handicap. In some cases these people become trustees, or attend fundraising events. In other cases, such as Comic Relief, the charities involved have found that sending a celebrity to an area, for example a drought-affected region in Africa, helps television viewers to find some sympathy for the afflicted. In some cases, celebrities charge a fee for working with a voluntary group.

'In an ideal world, the public will respond to a crisis from a humanitarian point of view. But people who are not familiar with a faraway country will respond more readily if the situation is explained by a familiar face that is trusted and seen every day on the television. We videotaped interviews with many of the celebrities, so that we can market them later to other media.'
Amita Arya, press officer with the Disaster Emergency Committee.

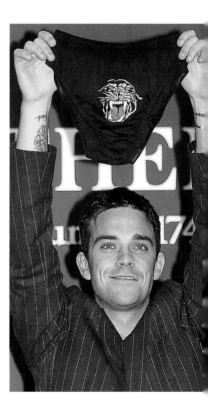

Pop singer Robbie Williams takes part in the Comic Relief fundraising day by auctioning his underwear. The event brings fun to television viewers and encourages them to donate money. But should we expect something in return for our donations to charity?

There is a personal value to be gained from volunteering. Apart from the pleasure of the activity, there is what is called the 'feel-good' factor. People feel happier and more content knowing they are helping others. Volunteering also offers experience in an area you might never have encountered had you not joined up. There is also the benefit of being able to write something positive about your out-of-school activities when filling in application forms for jobs and colleges. Some businesses now insist on employees completing a period of volunteering as part of their career package. This means that before they can continue with their careers, employees must complete a period of voluntary work, usually sponsored by the company.

Beneficiaries

You may already be the beneficiary of a voluntary group without knowing it. In schools, parent-teacher associations organize fundraising events for minibuses, computers, sports equipment and books. Your local community hall might be a registered charity, benefiting from the tax advantages of its charitable status.

A school parent teacher association holds a fundraising event. On an occasion such as this, parents and teachers meet, have fun line-dancing, and raise much-needed cash for school activities.

Millennium volunteering

In March 2000, the Labour government introduced a government-funded scheme whereby employees could take a day's paid leave once a year to do voluntary work. To get the scheme going, many members of the Cabinet and Downing Street and Cabinet Office employees took part, reading to children in local schools and nurseries and offering free legal aid for a day. The then Minister for Education, David Blunkett, spent the day in Sheffield at a Millennium Volunteer Project called 'Football Unite, Racism Divide'.

The government also plans to introduce a scheme called Experience Corps which would make it easier for retired people to do voluntary work. The Millennium Volunteer Project also offers funds for young people's voluntary activities. The Prime Minister, Tony Blair, said: 'I know a number of major companies are intending to embrace the scheme to allow their staff to take a day off, paid, once a year, to work in the voluntary sector. I intend to do this myself, both as an individual and as an employer, with people in Downing Street and the Cabinet Office able to take a minimum of one day's paid leave a year to do voluntary work. I hope many will take up this opportunity and I hope they will take it up throughout the country.'

David Blunkett (centre), ex-Minister for Education, visits a school in Sheffield in 2000 to launch the government's parents and schools project.

Activity

How to take part in the voluntary sector

1. Find a cause you believe in. There are many listings of charities, both on the internet and in libraries, where you can get an idea of local and national voluntary groups and what their needs are.

2. Behave ethically. Beyond giving your time in a voluntary group, there are many more things you can do to help good causes. Ethical shopping means only buying from a company with a good record as an employer. There are ethical shopping web sites on the internet. Try 'life shifting' – encourage your family to make less impact on the environment by recycling, composting vegetable waste, buying things with less packaging, using energy more economically. Become a blood donor, and fill out an organ donor card.

3. Campaign. To find out what it is like to take part in a campaign, find a topic at your school to campaign about. Are there issues to do with school dress, bullying, lunchtime activities, something the school needs but cannot afford?

Becoming involved in voluntary work helps you to feel better about yourself and understand other people's needs. Above: volunteer members of the International Children's Conference, Debbie Simmons and Dermot Bryers, set off from Heathrow airport to present a challenge document to United Nations leaders in New York.

You might wish instead to campaign on a national issue, such as blood sports, animal testing, or the age at which you are allowed to take a driving test.

4. Organize your campaign. First of all, decide on your aims. Consider the following questions:
• Who will be the beneficiary of your campaign?
• Does your campaign meet a real need?
• How do you know that this need exists?

5. Get some support. Your campaign will be much easier to carry out if you have the moral support of the people around you, so you need to start canvassing. Make a list of possible supporters and ask them for an interview so that you can explain your cause. Practical support is another important asset. You might need to make leaflets, carry out surveys, count ballots. A team of interested and committed fellow students is essential. Explain your campaign to as many people as possible by giving interviews, distributing leaflets, perhaps making a few speeches. Then see how many people you have persuaded to support your campaign by asking them to sign a petition. Good luck!

These children are doing their own voluntary work on behalf of the environment by recycling waste.

Glossary

advocacy arguing in favour of a cause

AIDS auto-immune deficiency syndrome – an illness that destroys a person's ability to fight off infection

almshouse a privately run and financed home for the poor

Alzheimer's disease a disease that slowly attacks brain cells, causing a gradual loss of memory and leaving the sufferer unable to manage simple everyday tasks

anti-capitalism demonstrations demonstrations in which the participants protest against the power and influence of multinational private companies

anti-personnel landmines shrapnel-filled bombs buried just under the surface of the ground, set to be triggered when some-one steps on them

anti-tank landmines landmines that are designed to explode when a tank passes over them

beneficiaries people who receive some benefit or help from an action

bloodsports sports such as hare-coursing, deer-hunting or fox-hunting, which involve the death of an animal

capitalism an economic system in which industry and property are owned by individuals or by large organizations rather than by the government

Common Law British law established by custom rather than by parliamentary laws

cystic fibrosis an inherited illness which causes breathing and digestive problems and, eventually, death

endowment a gift, usually of money or property

ethical campaigning campaigning on a moral or ethical issue, for example, against capital punishment or for women's rights

foundation an organization with a large amount of money which it uses to provide funds for other organizations

grant a sum of money given to an individual or organization

grant-making trust a charity with the resources to give sums of money to voluntary groups, other charities, research institutions, hospitals etc.

hostel a place where people can stay temporarily and under supervision

housing association a privately run organization that provides homes for its members

multinational companies companies with branches in several different countries

non-statutory something that is not determined by law or government

Parliamentary democracy/system a system of government where people elect representatives to become Members of Parliament (MPs)

pension fund money that a business keeps in hand in order to pay its employees a pension when they retire

poll tax a tax of a fixed annual amount which every adult must pay, regardless of income

social security a system in which an employer or the government provides medical care, pensions and other services for its employees or citizens

sponsorship the act of providing money or backing for some activity or event

time management planning your available time carefully

trustee a member of a group that has been given the power of administration of some company or property, with special orders as to how they must administer it

unsolicited mail letters which arrive in the post but have not been asked for

Value Added Tax a tax on the profits made when something is bought

voluntary sector those voluntary groups, charities and businesses that exist to help people rather than to make a profit

Resources

Books about individual charities and voluntary groups include:

Emily Wood, *The Red Cross Story*, Dorling Kindersley, 1995
Elspeth Clayton and Louise Spilsberg, a series of books on Barnardo's, Greenpeace, Help the Aged, Friends of the Earth, Oxfam and the National Society for the Prevention of Cruelty to Children, published by Heinemann

For a list of charities and voluntary groups, try:
Charities Digest 2001
International Voluntary Work, Whetter and Pybus, Vacation Work, 2000

Relevant web sites include:

http://www.ncvo-vol.org.uk/ the web site of the National Council for Voluntary Organizations, which has information on the latest events in the voluntary sector and a list of volunteering opportunities

http://www.bbc.co.uk/education/timebank another list of opportunities for volunteering

http://www.blood.co.uk/ the web site of the National Blood Donors Association

http://www.argonet.co.uk/body/ this web site gives advice on how to become an organ donor

http://www.ethicalconsumer.org/ this web site looks at the environmental record of some brand-named goods

http://www.getethical.com/ an ethical shopping site with online shopping for fair-trade, organic and energy-saving items

http://www.oneworld.net/ an online magazine with articles about issues concerning the developing world

http://www.greenchoices.org/ a magazine with information on environmentally sound things to buy

http://www.traidcraft.co.uk/ an online shop with a children's and schools' section

http://oxfam.org.uk/ an online, fair-trade shop with a schools' section

http://www.rprogress.org/ a web site where you can find a program to measure your ecological footprint; this shows the proportion of the world's resources you take up compared to people in other countries

http://www.saveenergy.co.uk/ a web site with information about how to save energy

For individual charities, try one of the search engines and type in the name of the charity or voluntary organization you are interested in.

Visit www.learn.co.uk for more resources.

Index